Elizabeth Cannell
Toronto
Aug' 2012

no narrative

PRISM

David St. John

with photographs by
Lance Patigian

Arctos Press

PRISM
A HoBear Publication

Copyright © 2002 by David St. John
Photographs © 2002 by Lance Patigian

All rights reserved. No part of this book may be reproduced or transmitted in any form or by any means, electronic or mechanical, including photocopying, recording or by an information storage and retrieval system without written permission from the author, and/or the artist except for the inclusion of brief quotations in a review.

ISBN 0-9657015-7-3

Library of Congress Control Number: 2002105353
Library of Congress Cataloging-in-Publication Data
1. Poetry 2. St. John, David - Poetry
3. United States - 21st Century - Poetry

First Edition

Acknowledgements
Some of these poems first appeared in the following magazines: *Alaska Quarterly Review, Art Life, Blackbird, The Blue Moon Review, Green Mountains Review, Kestrel, The Lyric, PoetryBay, Rivendell, RUNES, A Review of Poetry, The Southern Review, Washington Square,* and *West Branch.*
My thanks to the editors of these journals.

Book design by Jeremy Thornton
Front and back cover photographs by Lance Patigian

ARCTOS PRESS
P.O. Box 401
Sausalito, CA 94966-0401
CB Follett: Publisher
Runes@aol.com
http://members.aol.com/Runes

For Phil & Fran Levine

with love
David & Lance

I would like to thank Toni Burge, CB Follett, Susan Terris, and Susan Shreve for their guidance and support in the making of this collection.

DAVID ST. JOHN

David St. John's most recent collections are
STUDY FOR THE WORLD'S BODY:
New & Selected Poems (Harper Collins, 1994),
THE RED LEAVES OF NIGHT (Harper Collins, 1999), and
IN THE PINES: Lost Poems, 1972-1997, (White Pine, 1998).

His many prizes include The Rome Fellowship in Literature and an Academy Award in Literature, both from The American Academy of Arts and Letters, and the O. B. Hardison Prize in Poetry, awarded by The Folger Shakespeare Library.

LANCE PATIGIAN

Lance Patigian is a poet and photographer who currently divides his time between Carmel, California and Tucson, Arizona. Richard Nilson of *The Arizona Republic* describes his work as "marvelous... stunningly well made... and it stands out like a string quartet at a tractor pull."

CONTENTS

THE OPAL TREES 1
TURQUOISE 11
SAFFRON 13
BLUE NAILS 15
BLOOD ORANGES 17
ABSINTHE 19
LE RAYON VERT 21
STATEMENT OF STYLE 23
CHESTNUT 25
PRISM 27
    I.   ICE 27
    II.   RED PYTHON 29
    III. SEPIA: NOSTALGIA SONG 31
    IV. BUMBLE BEE 33
    V.   MEDITERRANEAN MINT 35
    VI. GENTIANS 37
    VII. THISTLE 39
    VIII. RAVEN'S HOOD 41
COAST POPPIES 51
PINK NACRE 53
SMOKING IN HAVANA 55
CORAL SHALLOWS 57
BLUE NAILS (II) 59
PASTE 61
TUMBLEWEEDS 63
PEACH FIRES 65

WOODY	67
VERONA	69
BLACKBERRY	71
FATIGUE	73
UPTOWN GIRL (JUNIPER BERRY)	75
MANHATTAN DIPTYCH	77
I. BLACK LIGHT	77
II. GOLDEN SHOWERS	79
TIMBERWOLF	81
BRICK	91
BLACK LIGHT (II)	93
CERISE	95
BUTTERSCOTCH: A SONG (Carpe Diem)	97
THE SHADOWS OF LYME	99
LOTUS QUEEN	101
PORNO PINK	103
BRANDY	105
GLACIER	107
BURNT SIEN(N)A	109
ST. CLARE'S BODY	111
NERO	113
ISABELLA	115
THE GYPSY'S QUILT	117
MURK	119
PRISM (WHITE LIGHT)	121

PRISM

THE OPAL TREES

When I awaken into the dream

Of your body upon my body
I am breathing the fragrant air of
The opal trees where shivering rags
Of light pearlesque the limbs of
Your body upon my body
As I awaken to the moonscape

Of this solitary bed
Still feeling the soft satin of stone
& the blossoms of the opal trees
Littering the sheets of earth beneath me
As their shattered rinds
Swirl through the branches of the dream

Of your body upon my body

TURQUOISE

Imagine the sky compressed within
The clenched earth

The pressure composed by deep fire
At the core of

The ether of transcendence surrounding
Us until the knuckles & nuggets

Spit high into the air
A smoldering blessing

Of the involuted skies as if even
The light above the sea had folded

Back onto itself so many times
This petrified mirror of stone we carry

Becomes a bible   blue
Darkening from beauty into night

SAFFRON

Even the thin tube of Spanish saffron
Sitting on the spice rack above the butcher block
Cooking table seems to glow with the worth
Of at least its weight in gold & today
At the beach a dozen Buddhist monks in golden
Robes stepped out of three limousines
To walk their Holy One out along the dunes

To the water's flayed edge where the sand burned
With a light one could only call in its reddish
Mustard radiance the essence of saffron
& what I remember most of the scene as
The Holy One knelt down to touch those waves
Was his sudden laughter & his joy & that
Billowing burnt lemon light opening across the sky

BLUE NAILS

They were piled on his workshop table
Like little mountains of exclamation points
    Inked silver-blue & drying
Discarded by some disgruntled printer
Who'd long since left this village
For a city with streetlights
& paving stones while his brother stayed

Here where the workshop light grew dim
Early in the winter but business was surely good
    & lately blooming with the lesions
Along the bodies of the villagers he'd
Always lived among though one by one they'd
Come to see him laid out on planks while
He assembled each coffin nail by single blue nail

end of Sept.

BLOOD ORANGES

An empty cafe in Sirmione
The stone terrace almost derelict
In the off season the harsh winter winds

Whipping up the white caps on Lake Garda

& still she brings him the juice
Of the blood oranges
So incongruous in the cool brisk silence

Of early morning where only the peculiar clang

Of the metal rowboat knocking against the small
Hotel dock marks off the time one
Believes is passing

However languidly however without regard

To what might be truly necesssary even essential
To the odd solitary questing of one hapless
If hopeful man

ABSINTHE

There is nothing like it in nature
No leaf so iridescent in its gleam just

Think of the way light passes through
The glass on the cafe table firing

The air around it with the fierce
Current of the brain corroding back

To its own nature which is
To say this animal hunger rising

Through the flesh & visionary hopes
Of the whole assembled tableau of

Losers derelicts actors saltimbanques
Painters widows thieves who populate

A century lit by this glass finger-lantern
Of glowing rage

Aug 13, 2012
Toronto

LE RAYON VERT

Movies books rumors everywhere
We're all talking about *le rayon vert*
That streak that taut line of light
Flashing the green of the afterlife

For only a moment just at sunset
The surprise of the instant of the electric
Lime ribbon snapping along the curved
Edge of the horizon past the pallid waves

& cruise ships in the harbor
& the boys in jeans eyeing the girls in bikinis
Where the rasping heat has scrubbed the brain
Of all pretense of intelligence

& only the most elemental of our desires
Survives the click of the lid of the coming night

STATEMENT OF STYLE

She gave a whole new meaning to the phrase
Seeing red the way even the sheets
& curtains & mahogany table conspired
To enwomb you in that pulsing web of
Heat & of course if I'd any sense at all
I'd have been out of there

In twenty seconds but such scarlet convictions

I admit held for me a certain allure so
I continued to read aloud from my
Favorite translation of Reverdy as she
Undressed me with no little humor & much
Determination until it was clear I was very much
In the pink as they say but oh my Lord not

At all out of those red woods

CHESTNUT

A silver mist hung along the Paris street
As she walked wrapped in a brown cloak woven
Some years before she was born & at

The corner of the *Rue de l'Odeon*
A chestnut seller stood holding out to her
A paper cone of split nuggets

Hot *marrons* & as she thought of the Ardèche
& those distant gnarled limbs of her childhood
She passed over a few francs then held her face

Above the dark steaming stones warming her lips
A moment before prying open one of the
Hard fruits with her raw fingers

Then sucking the searing gray meat onto her
Tongue where her familiar silence had only
A moment ago so precariously hung

PRISM

I. ICE

All diamond I'd thought & no rough
The white-blonde shadows along the bed
Like shifting pillows of snow made flesh
& in the delicate if excruciating ballet of

Departure it's hard not to recall the snow leopard
Rubbing her cool flanks against the silver bars
As I watched hypnotized & wholly taken
Not yet knowing the broken have no choice

In the end but to run & so tonight pouring
Harsh Spanish brandy over the opaque
Squares rattling in my glass I can only think
Of the judgment my Eastside Princess ex-lover gave

In her best pimp-voice (about this new love) testifying —
Boy now you just remember . . . *that* fukkin bitch is *cold*

II. RED PYTHON

I didn't see it until she stretched out
One leg as she shifted her weight
On the chair at the conference table where
We'd been discussing some detail so arcane

Even the academic horseshit flies had grown bored

& beneath the steel grey silk of that pant leg
Flicked quick as a tongue a single razor-toed boot
Scaled unmistakably with the stripped skin
Of some sacred serpent slicked still
& dyed the same shade as

The memory of some ancient sacrifice where
The stones themselves had grown bloody as hope
& as I caught her eye for just an instant

I felt all that useless human breath squeezed out of me

III. SEPIA: NOSTALGIA SONG

Everything's worse than it was
Even faded & distant & rinsed in the faint

Tea of history
The past is more glorious than the world today

Those worries & constant percussive proclamations
Of urgency & importance we import into

Our daily lives oh even
The bitterness of love is given the tint of dried

Blood across the landscape of our
Final desire to be safely again anywhere *any*where

But here oh please most especially not *here* or there
Where the vague mirage of hope meets

The fabulous failure of an evening in our shimmering
Breakdown of embrace

IV. BUMBLE BEE

It was such a Fifties kind of thing
The astonishing sport coat at the back
Of the drop-dead expensive Roman men's store
I'd passed by almost every day just off

The Corso & sure enough it was exactly
My size & it's almost impossible to describe
The vibrating sense of pleasure
The soft lines of alternating butter-&-black

Gave to the haze left in the eye of
The gazer in this case meaning me as I stood
Before the mirror
Smoothing the lapels along my swelling chest

& the woman beside me herself just a little
Breathless turned & said, "Oh honey, oh honey...."

V. MEDITERRANEAN MINT

She gathered a fistful of
Mint from her small hillside garden
Where the single goat stood lazily munching
& slapping flies off his back with the rope of his tail

& she leaned above the pit of blushing coals
Where the leg of lamb hissed up at her
& sprinkled the bruised flakes over it as lightly
As a goddess dispensing her virginal grace & it was

The certain heat of the day rising off the bland sheen
Of the jade water he would remember most
Just that & the way her skin later that evening
Still damp with sweat smelled hot as lamb

& cypress just as her fingers in his open mouth
Tasted of the faint chartreuse of bloody summer mint

VI. GENTIANS

Every descent is a promise that one
Will arise in some far better place — oh dear
Lost again to the pomegranate seed
Bring back the purple torch & light our season
Jesus you'd think we'd know better by now
The descent is *only* the descent beckoning
My dear doctor like a well reflecting sky

The purity of the ascent opening to fate
For a few of us whose emblazoned desires
Blossom like spring which echoes the vast
Hilarity of the underworld as the satyrs
Romp in sweet abandon & the maenads
Await the return of their favorite rock star
Dear Orpheus still looking over your own shoulder....

VII. THISTLE

No downy crown of thorns only the passions
Blown wildly violet in the dawn mist

The shock of stiff bristles uplifted
To the first failed affections of the sun

& if this is Palm Sunday then one must
Assume (& bear) the woven reed cross fanning

The exhausted madre shepherding her brood
Across the uneven brown stones of the plaza

Into the sanctuary cool of the sacred dark
Where almost imperceptibly heads

Turn to note the one slim son whose hair
Is dyed the deep purple of punk saints & some

Nod in mild approval some sneering stonily as we
Look up into the light where soon all shall be risen again

VIII. RAVEN'S HOOD

As if the night itself were masked

The skeen of sweat polishing the leather
Restraints set off by thin silver chains
Criss-crossing her body so that the scarred

Relief of her skin glowed in the candle light
Like the first sacrament of a ritual given
Over to the pain of desire

As the pleasure of the torn aperture
Released the whole negative of the image
All in black-&-white the slick raven's hood

Pulled down to just above his lips which
She touched just once with a gloved finger
Before she turned her back to him & let

The claws of love begin to sing

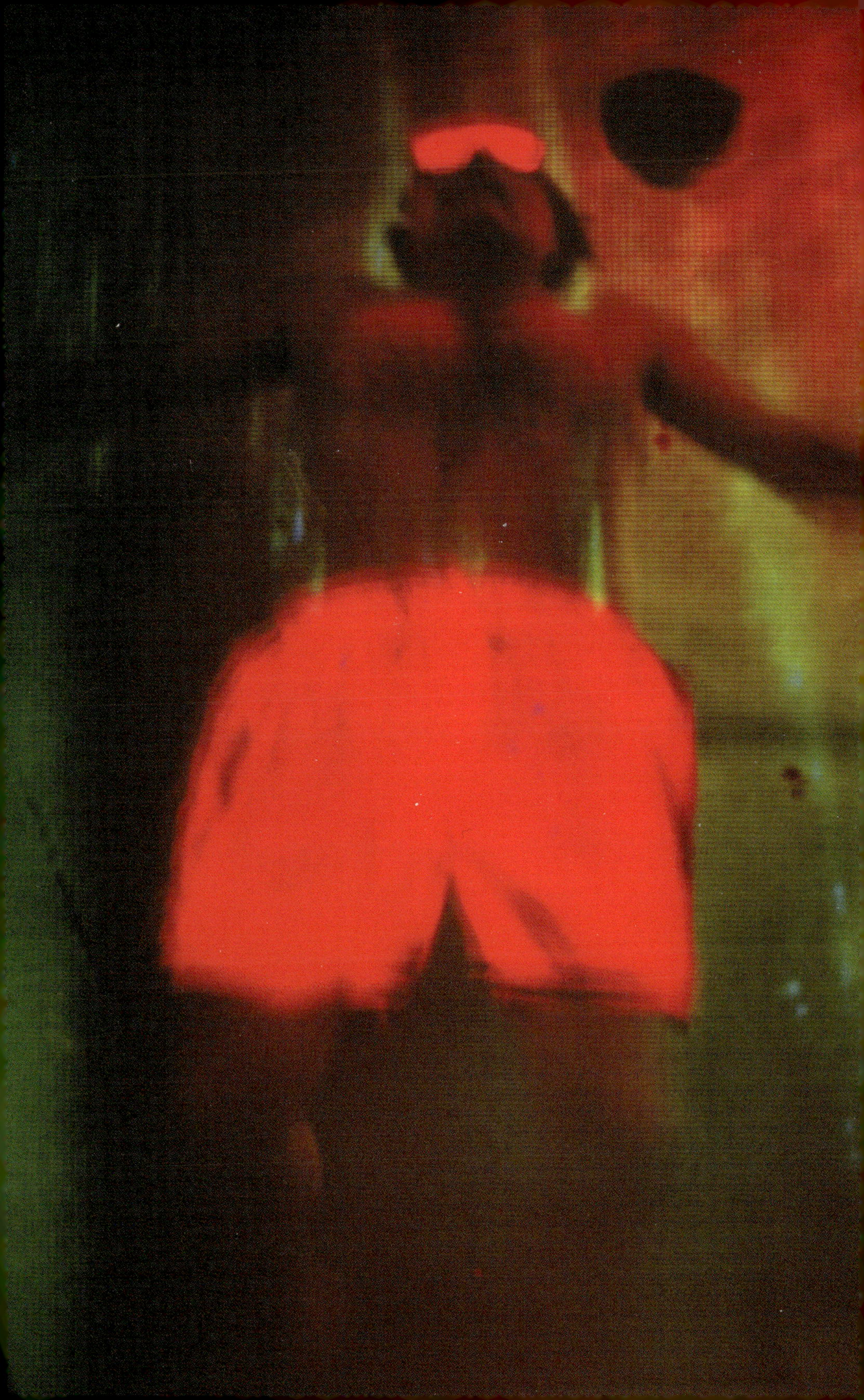

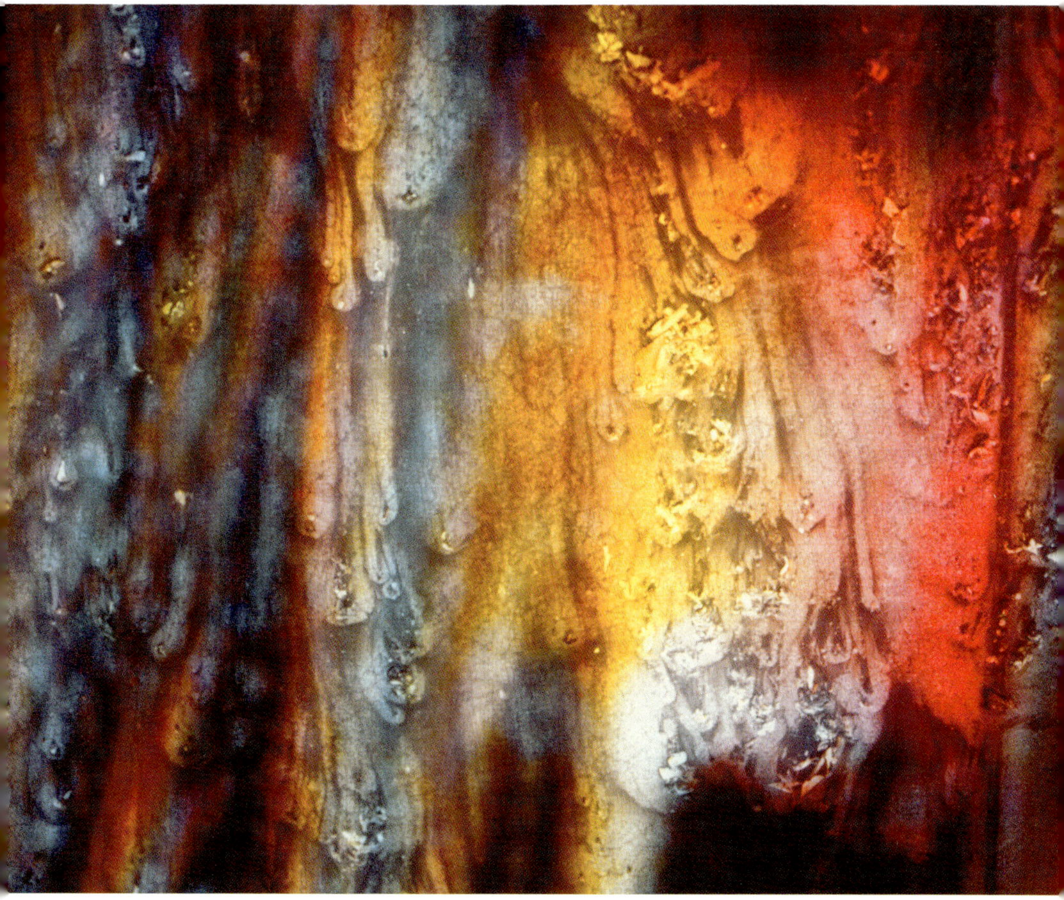

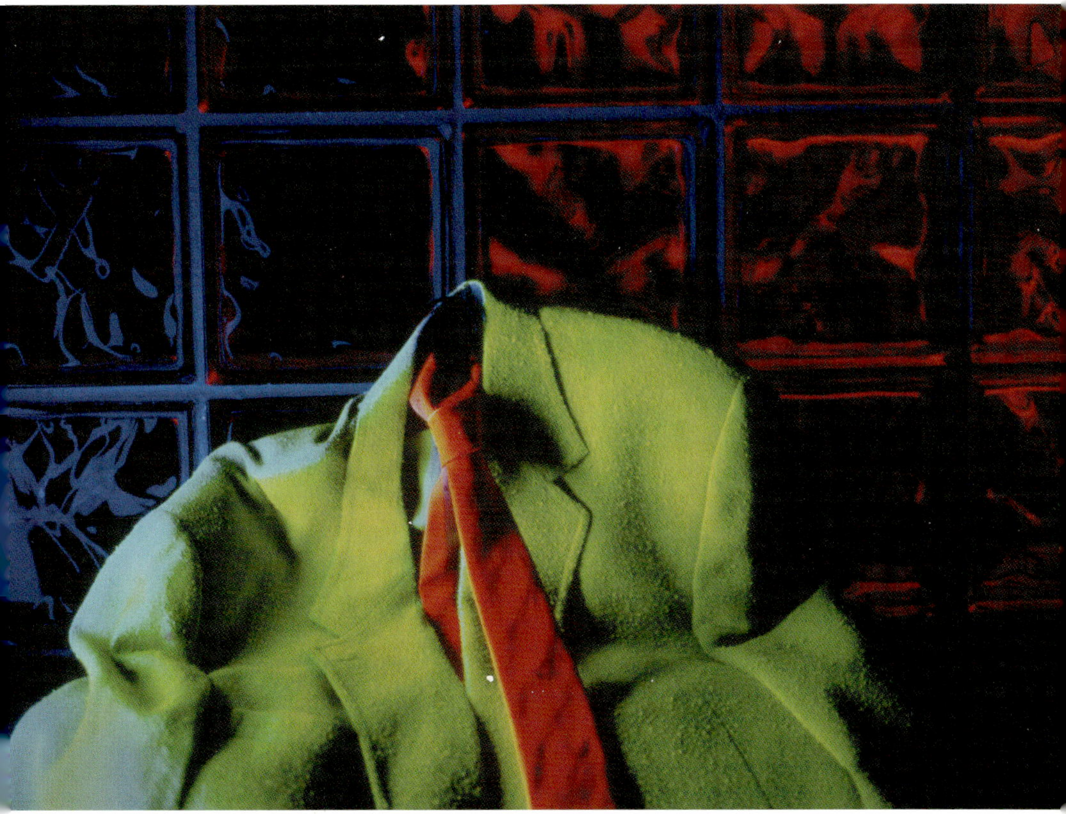

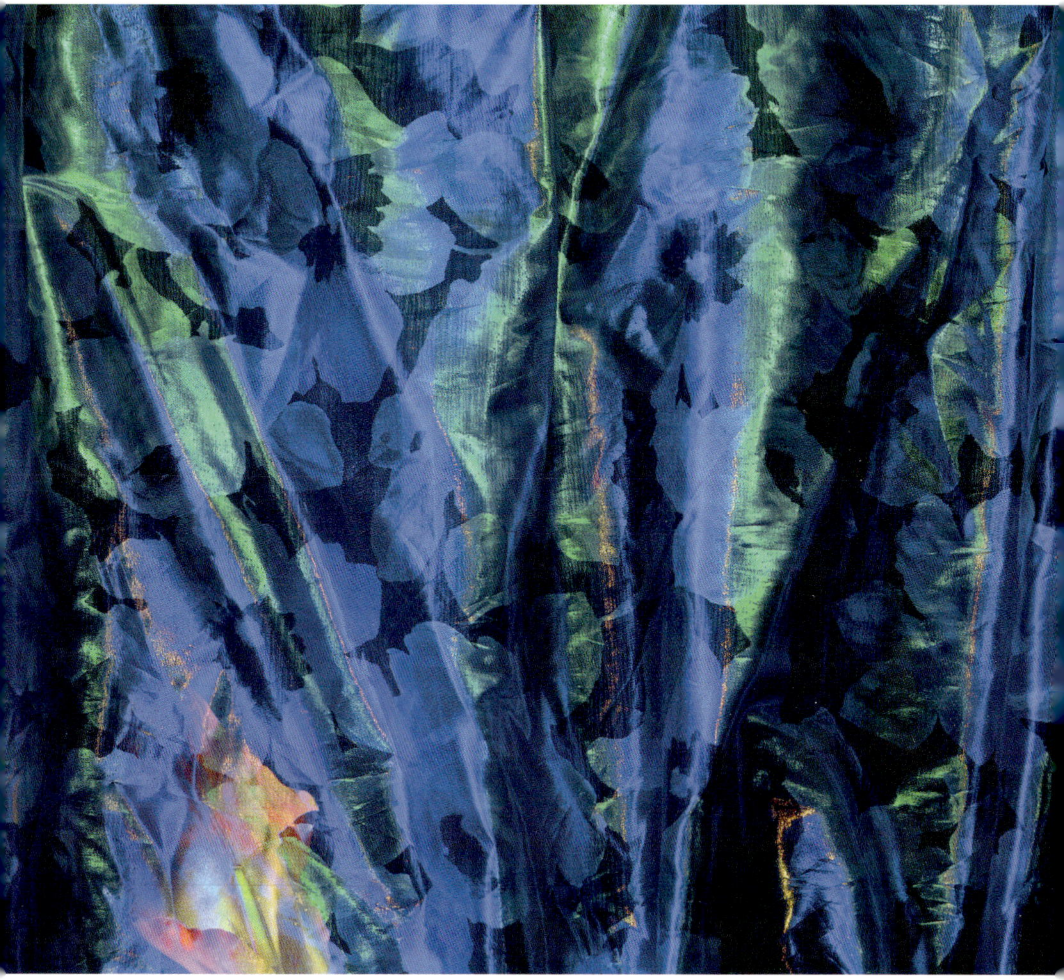

COAST POPPIES

The sea air blues the sheer cliffs
Rising up from the shaggy foam below
To these narrow terraces of blowing orange masks
Tiny paper faces nodding on their stalks
& as we walk the snaking muddy trail above

The Pacific waves shattering
Against the rocks along the fringe of Little Sur

I want to gather those fields of paper bells
Swaying like fragile Japanese lanterns yes
Just gather as we pass a whole basket
Of crenelated orange lips into my arms
& bury you in them until every move you'd make

Would rustle like this summer breeze
& the soft laughter of poppies

PINK NACRE

Like the northern lights
Along the pearled half-moon of

The inner abalone as the old Chumash
Woman smashes the edge of its shell
Against the flat stone until the muscle
Of hinge snaps open & the flat mucus meat
Shines like dirty snow in the afternoon

Sunlight as the small girl

At her side waits patiently to rinse
Those precious lights in the rock tidepool
Filling as the tide recedes   as she waits to
Splinter those hard liquid rainbows
Into jagged pieces she'll string on a single thread of

Woven grass to wear like teeth like jewels across her chest

SMOKING IN HAVANA

This is how he'd always seen himself
Even afterwards when the world knew better

He was he knew in his heart the man
Standing at the balcony of the villa

Built in the 30s for some Latin starlet
Who'd died too young they said from love

& heroin the stakes of both being suitably high
& as he stood looking out over the bay

At the light rising in narrow flat panes
Over the blank waves he took out a cigar

Twice the length of his hand & held to its fat dulled tip
A stick match he'd drawn from his velvet

Evening jacket & scraped across the sky — just the way
Fate begins with every dumb false god

CORAL SHALLOWS

Marble angel are you still there standing
On the coral beach in Key West calling me on
Your cell phone to say I'm sorry it was all just another

Misunderstanding one of so many we seem to be
Having lately as those quaint tongues of death creep
Up the legs of our own shadows but for my part

I keep my talismans close — my necklace with
Its wing of silver lit by turquoise & red coral
& obsidian which the old woman in the pueblo

Fastened around my neck saying You are a creature
Of blood inflamed as coals & this wing will
Lift you above the fields of sorrow

She really said that & you said So here I am 3,000 miles
Away beside shallows reeking of green primeval sex

BLUE NAILS (II)

Circumstance means everything when
Night begins to creep closer to the bed
& silence is the worst lover not to

Mention the most wasteful so she sat

At her dresser naked from the waist
Up & held out first her left hand then
Her right each with a slow consideration

As if she were watching five moons rise

Now from the East & now the West
Each pale oval lacquered a nervous blue
The same neon pulse as certain tropical fish

In the clear shallows of the Caribbean where
Certainly she would one day be living in her next
& more deeply gracious life

PASTE

The sickening opacity of an egg frying
On the skillet until the white
Clouds to a sticky viscous state
Its milky gelatinous ooze   a sunny sludge

But the purest glob of reality remains in that jar
Just put back upon the shelf of the classroom
At day's end those lumps of school paste
Tasty & sour but ever so useful

With its wooden tongue depresser of a stick
Absently tossed out with the trash
As the teacher clears the work table for the last
Of several times & she lifts the hope as she turns

Out the lights that at least something in her life
For once might simply hold & be held

TUMBLEWEEDS

At six the empty lots of my block
Still held those shocked balloons of tumbleweeds —
The land was still that new to any use

& I dug pits eight feet across then ringed them
With the spiny balls wrenched from their roots
A defense against community not often enough
Appreciated in this day & age & I wonder if

When X sang *Tumblin' Tumbleweeds* at the edge of
Chesapeake Bay or when M sweetly gave me
The CD of Gene Autry singing that classic
As I hum along I wonder if either of them

Ever knew how close they'd come to touching
The soft center of that boy's fort
Forever held & wildly defended even to this very day

PEACH FIRES

Out in the orchards the dogs stood

Almost frozen in the bleak spring night
& Mister dragged out into the rows
Between his peach trees the old dry limbs

Building at regular intervals careful pyres
While the teeth of the dogs chattered & snapped
& the ice began to hang long as whiskers

From the globes along the branches
& at his signal we set the piles of branches ablaze
Tending each carefully so as not to scorch

The trees as we steadily fed those flames
Just enough to send a rippling glow along
Those acres of orchard where that body —

Sister Winter — had been held so wisely to the fire

WOODY

Don't be vulgar it's not at all
What you think — I mean of course only

A station wagon with its sides panelled
In banana-yellow wood grained

As smoothly as a surfer's ancient longboard
Poking out of the open window of the rear hatch

& the liquid gold along its flanks
Makes the woody both resolute & sexy

At the same time as the girl slides behind the wheel
To drive him home after a day of burns & waves

& pleasure & salt left caked along their mouths
Just as tonight when the moonlight blanks

The open windows of their bedroom he'll lick the salt
Off her lips as deliberately as any animal happy in its pain

VERONA

In France it is the midnight naval
Blue of workmen's clothes the heavy canvas
Of their stiff pants & square jackets
A blue edging almost to black
In its purity though not like
Ink more like the sky gathering its evening
Basket of stars & here at dusk in Verona

The nightly *passeggiata* brings out the gentlemen
Of the city   so measured & self-possessed in their
Calm & pleasure as their wives
Carefully hook arms in theirs   each Signore
Wrapped in a wool hued so richly even God's sheep
Must be ashamed to be so lost in its deep indigo ah
But the men of course look glorious   & amused

BLACKBERRY

It is time I believe we all confessed
That every blackberry in our poetry

Begins on the hedge of Francis Ponge's
Delicious page each American blackberry

Plucked from the French thicket of his prose
The ink of each letter the squib of the nib

The pen scrawled in the raw cursive of
The blackberry its squid-sweet succulence

The poem's own viscous evil given a form
So pleasing to the tongue its hive

Of planets huddled close into a tight cosmos
Of utter darkness though the righteous are often

Discouraged by those asterisks of thorns
Which poets prefer truly to the fruit

FATIGUE

So drab tonight even the moon

Glows the shade of a winter olive
& the camouflage of leaves upon shadows
Upon leaves falls along the city street

Where she's dressed to kill in that surplus

Style carved head to toe with military irony
Her jacket with its hunter's ghostliness
Of browns & emeralds open & naked almost

To her waist & the red silk scarf at her throat

Could be a kind of wound
If the arrows of the night fly true
& she can muster the attention to stay

A bit longer at the party she'll soon

Arrive at only to recognize nearly everyone
There with an ever growing & simply devastating
Fatigue

UPTOWN GIRL (JUNIPER BERRY)

Of all the gin joints in all the . . .
Of course we know the rest the close
Terror of love lost brought home again

Scouring our tongues with rancor
& regret as we pronounce aloud the names
Of every reason we were betrayed

Those intimate pursed lips of refusal
Mouthing all over again the distance
To be crossed between her desires & your

Desires as if the last cab in the naked city
Refused to leave Soho tonight
The driver passed out at the wheel

The subway flash-flooded with summer rains
& you're alone in your cups again

MANHATTAN DIPTYCH

I. BLACK LIGHT

It wasn't enough he was in love
With Ultra Violet after seeing her once
In the Warhol spread in *Ramparts*
No he actually if accidentally ran into her
In the street outside *Max's Kansas City*
In the twisted early hours just before dawn & heaven
Which he said later never looked closer as

She dragged him along with her friends
This sick new puppy from the sticks
With nothing to recommend him but his job
At Bergdorf's & his good looks
& sensational tan which he soon discovered
Looked in the black light of the night's party
As if he'd been painted with chocolate wax

II. GOLDEN SHOWERS

It was one of those old claw-footed tubs
That sit in the middle of the kitchen
In ancient Manhattan apartments usually
Covered by a board to help disguise
Such cramped utility & all the lights
In the place were off so she was lit
Only by the pulsing neon of the various
Signs hung along the side of her building
& the one opposite
     each flashing name signifying
Some virtue on the street below & she sat naked
Then reclining in the tub as I stood
Inside it & above her & as she closed her eyes
In something like rapture she teased again
"Ok asshole, now piss on me...."

TIMBERWOLF

Arctic manners serve some of us well by
Which I mean a coolness edging to the predatory

But it's no way to lead a life said my old pal
The albino werewolf as we were out strolling

The lake's lip one evening & I can tell
He's upset so I say Look man you're famous

For doing half the models in the Hamptons
& the Paris/Berlin twins to boot (so to speak) so

Do you mean to tell me there's a heart
Softening in that corpse of ice you carry so elegantly

Along your beautiful thin bones & he seemed
Horrified he might actually be suspected of some

Feeling other than lust but then he smiled & said
Well but now you see I'm lonely as a stone

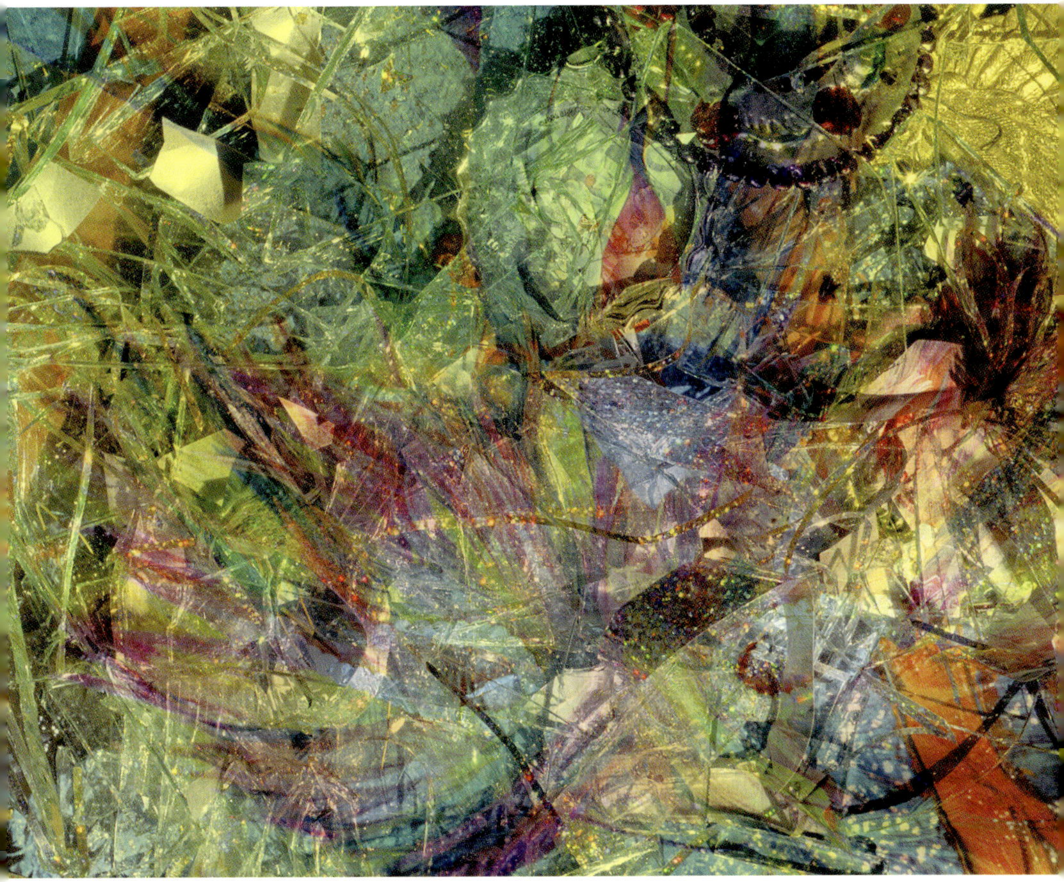

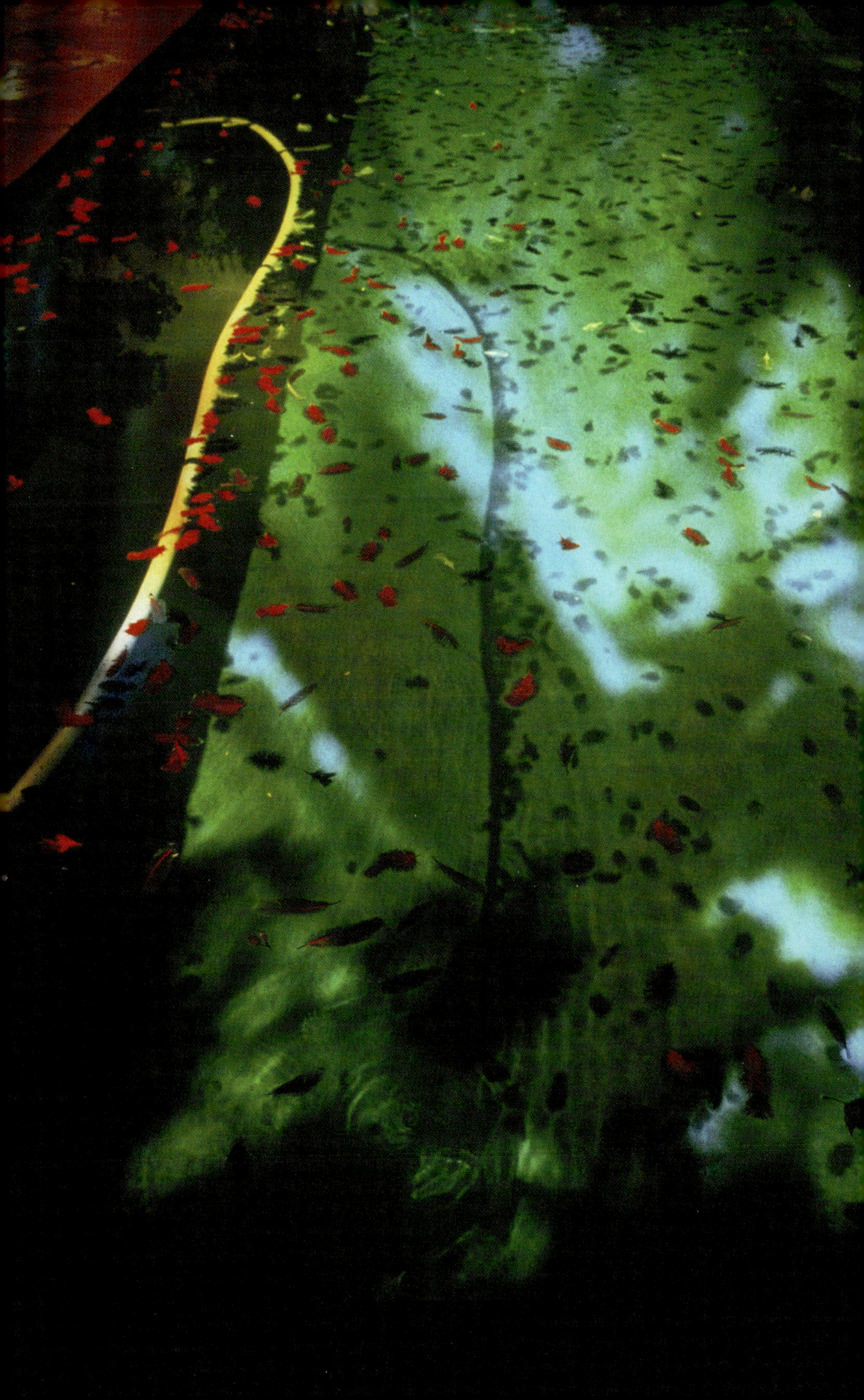

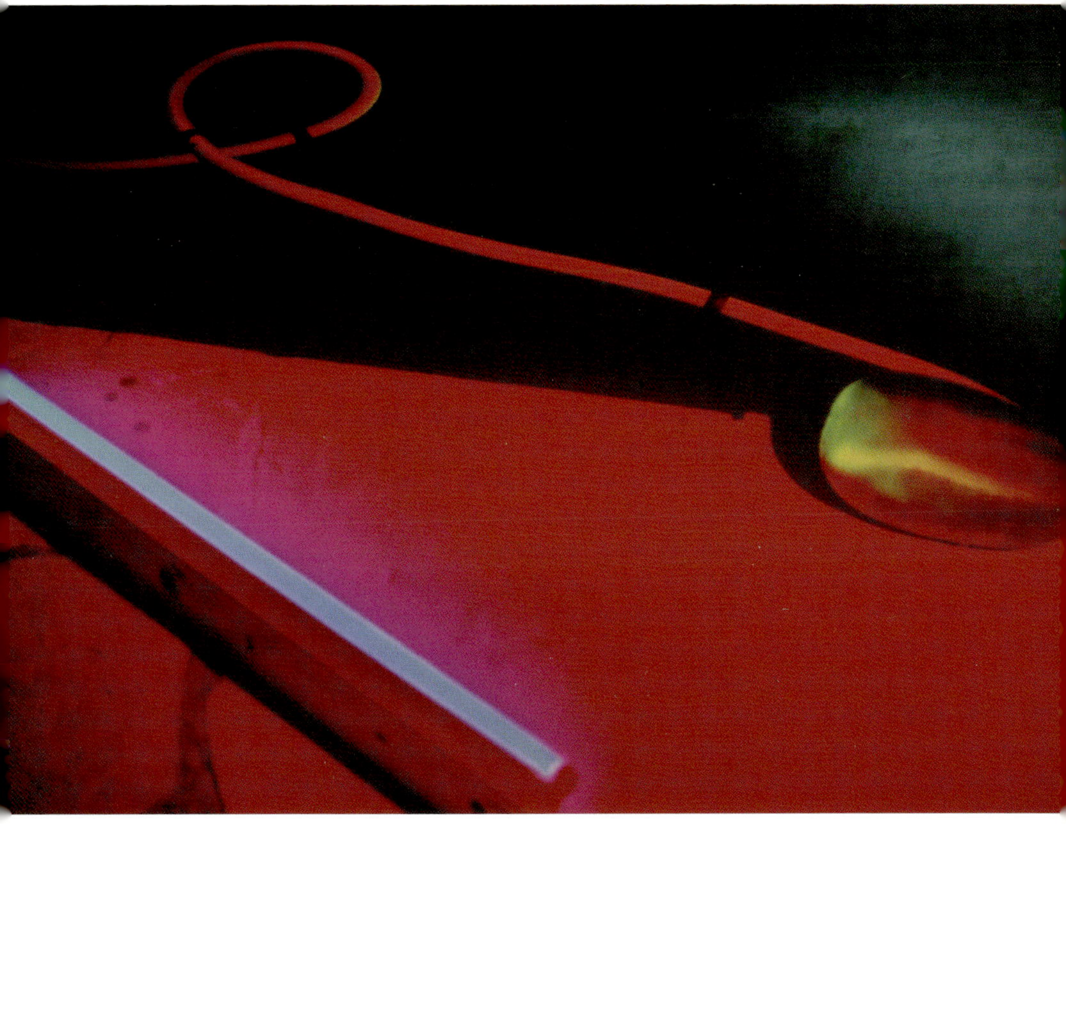

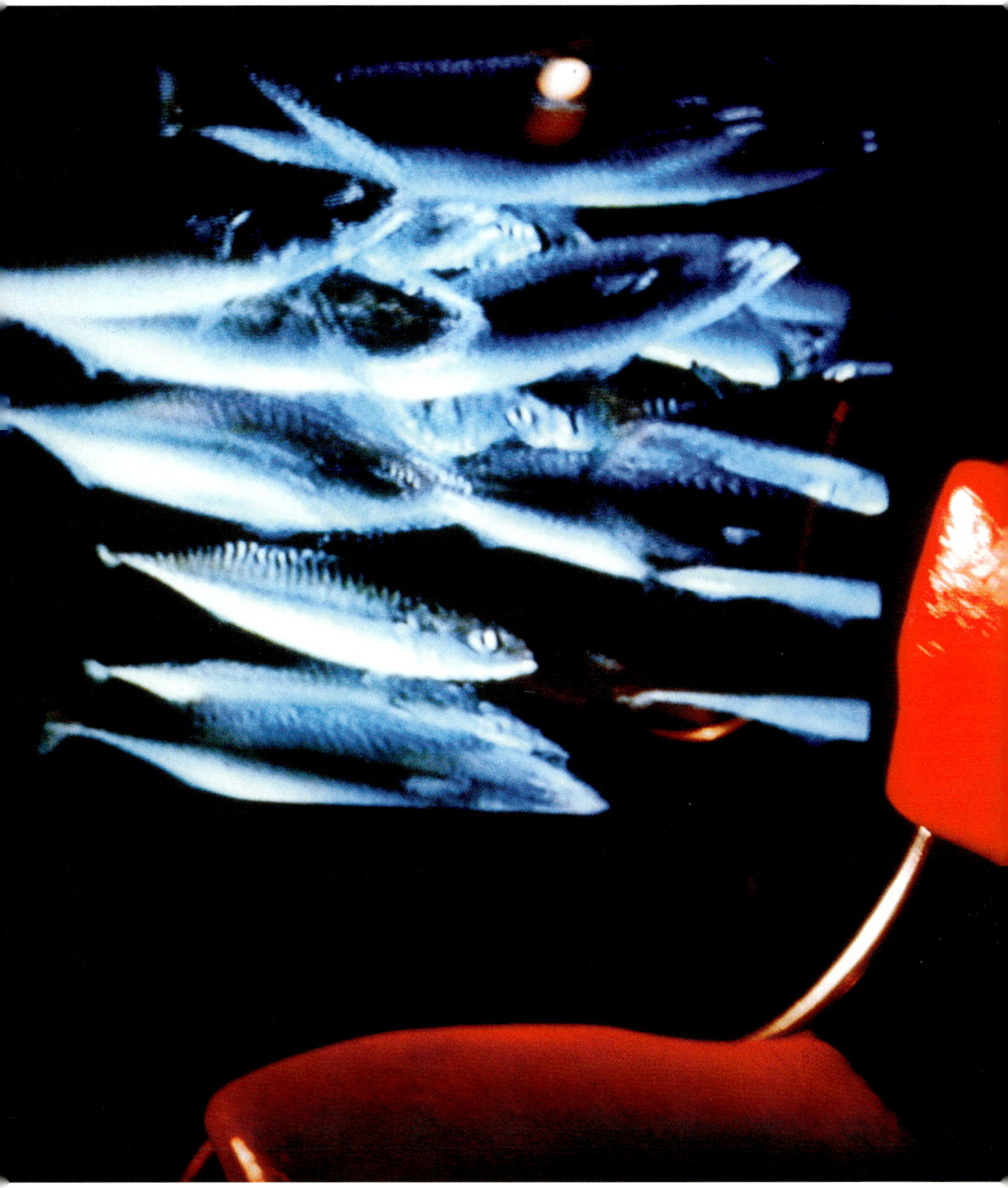

BRICK

In the endless blocks of dulled-blood
Brick rowhouses surrounding the few hills
Leading to the Baltimore Museum at the edge

Of Charles Village where the secrets of Hampton

Filtered through the legacies of families departed
Out of their Appalachian pasts some of them starch eaters
& some junkies with sons posing for the one

Neighborhood pornographer the money they made

Just enough to keep their mother in smack
A few more weeks then the cops came for
All of them & the dumb porches & the narrow stairways

& the closeness of people piled up on top of one another
In the summers as the Bay Seasoning & red cayenne pepper

Boiled the crabs the buttery color of brick

BLACK LIGHT (II)

He thought almost everything in the Sixties
Looked better under black light

Certainly his shitty room with its posters
Announcing the bending of consciousness almost

Beyond consciousness & the many deities
Of rock 'n' roll & he'd sit on the mattress

Stretched across the bare floor & roll her a joint
While pointing out the Tibetan prayer flags

Hung across the alley in his neighbor's window
& the violet dark of the room gave his nakedness

The kind of greenish pallor he'd desired
All of his life as if he were a creature

Who'd already passed to the other side & was just
Back briefly for this one short hour to receive

Her swift & uncomplicated love

CERISE

She was walking in the cherry orchard
& the moon washed the stiff folds
Of her gown with the misery of the century

& ah those blisters of consciousness bursting
All around her in the air like
Descartes' shooting stars piercing the blackening sky

As above her those dangling constellations of
Tiny cerise planets trembled
With the held expectations of the evening just past

As her life seemed to have passed
With its late knowledge of blood broken
Along the familiar sheets she'd gathered that morning

& shoved into the basement furnace where
The blaze of the flames breathed slowly & then deeply red

BUTTERSCOTCH: A SONG
(Carpe Diem)

Come darling come with me today
We'll walk the butterscotch heath
Along those narrow stone pathways
& drift in the new dawn's breath

Don't worry don't wonder we'll make
This passage dangerous & brief
& along those narrow pathways
We'll dance in the face of our deaths

So child come with me remember
The scent of the butterscotch heath
Your skin as bare as the summer's
Your hair a haloed wreath

We'll rise with the new dawn's breath
& dance in the face of our deaths

THE SHADOWS OF LYME

Restless as wind

Shallowed down over the stone jetty where
She walked toward the fronds of spray exploding

Off the storm waves & so   it was clear

I could only follow into that chaos of weather
Hoping to change something of the day

To change even her mind perhaps about

All of those catastrophes of circumstance
But of course such foolishness is rewarded

As it is always rewarded with nothing

But contempt followed by silence even
As the unfolding clouds split a moment while
The splayed light spread across the ground —

Uncertain shadows of the uncertain shivering leaves

LOTUS QUEEN

The bar had an aquarium that ran the whole
Length of one wall & everyone & everything

Hung a little underwater too in its dim & wavering light
So she & I would sit there

While the diners came & went from the Chinese restaurant
Attached next door & the ornate Oriental grillwork

& scuplted carving of the tables & the doors
Reminded me how simply delicate she

Seemed smelling always of sweet lotus oil & gin
& the white silk of her Mandarin blouse

Was stitched with those elaborate green leaves
& exquisite beige blossoms which she fingered

Gently as the smack worked its way through the veins
Of her pain & the night drew us close again

PORNO PINK

You could see the sign for miles along
The roadside advertising its special favors

For any traveller weary of the business
Of the world & more than ever prepared

To take some comfort from the extremity
Of others as well as their own special

Extremities including the sexual the sensual
The balls-out abandon of the crowd

Urging on the pole dancer to new heights
Of lubricious pink peformance

As those familiar glass flames of neon
Both above the bar & above the street burn

Describing the nature of a fire consuming
Even the least thirsty man in the room

BRANDY

In those days   my drink of
Choice all those lost hours that summer

Hanging out at the Deadwood afternoons & nights
& after hours killing time waiting for C

To get off her shift so we could go eat someting
Or drink some more & then sleep it off

& some days the brandy seemed to glow
With a brassy light radiating through the entire

Bar & at last through me as if some final
Buddhahood had been lit within my heat-

Scorched brain & then Norman would look up
Across the booth & sighing

Point at the glowing jukebox & say Man for
Christsakes will you just play P3

GLACIER

The ice-blue silk of her nightgown caught
The reflected light of the candles
She'd lit & set in a row along the ledge of
The open window where the chill
Breath of the early falling night arrived
Like the cool touch of the lace hem
He would remember passing along

His legs as she crawled on top of him
Running her lips over his nipples
Before pulling her legs close to his hips
The sheer glacier of the long gown slowly
Gathering up around her waist
As they entered those seas of transport
The polar caps rocking in their sudden steam

BURNT SIEN(N)A

It was a dream   but it felt to her then
Exactly like the world—

. . .the day of the Palio. . .& the Palio was in flames
The windows of every building framing the piazza

Rippling with the wind-stunned banners

& below the horses broke from the starting line
Breaking each into burnished flames
                              & the colors of each rider
Rose emblazoned upon the air

& caught the final republic of   wind
Sky   wood   the history of betrayal mixed

With the scent of charred horseflesh as she awoke
& he awoke to a day burning on their lips

Acrid as this wafer of ash

ST. CLARE'S BODY

It held all light & therefore

Was by definition the very absence of
Light & color & the black char

Of the limbs was also the ash of repose

The tree of night curled
Around itself until the blessings softened

Until even the heat lifted beyond

The gristle of cross
We will know her by those evenings

After midnight when almost asleep

We'll notice her there across the room
Resting perhaps & most certainly stretched out

On the narow settee worn bare by travellers

Who like you still search the dark
Of all Montefalco

NERO

The glint along the water of the canals
Of the few stars still visible as the clouds
Gather blackening the lagoon where the rows

Of gondolas rock side by side in the wash
Of the tide their necks crooked high
Above the narrow dock alongside Julietta's

Father's *palazzo* where the tiles of the windowsills
Begin to moisten with the morning dew & the lazy scarfs
Of mist twist & play along the humpbacked stone

Bridges as the cats take their turn navigating the city
As the French boy in Julietta's bedroom turns from the window
Where he's been standing the whole while waiting to ask

What do you *call*   the *black* of those gondolas?

ISABELLA

It is the nicotine-stained scarf of air
Wrapping the throat of the *Janicolo* at dusk
The night of the Academy's show of young Italian
Architects & through those hellish iron
Gates walked — still herself in mourning black —
The single most beautiful woman in the world so
Regal & measured as she moved through the *cortile*
— & she looked up
                    just for a moment
Holding my glance yet never slowing her steady death
March pace toward her family & duty as once indoors
She reached inside her black bag & first put on her mask
Of sunglasses & then pulled out a silk lemon handkerchief
Which flashed like a flame against her perfect pale face

THE GYPSY'S QUILT

It was the story she remembered best
From her grandmother when as a girl she'd
Slide into sleep beneath the pile of blankets
& the frayed dull-ivory quilt in the cold mountain
Cabin yes the one about that gypsy woman
Who one night arrived at their door
With a dead baby in her arms (not dead just drugged

They knew) begging her grandfather to buy
At least this precious white quilt wrapped around
The child oh that magical quilt woven of snow
& cobwebs spun she'd said by seven plump black widows
Which would now protect with her own's child death the life
Of any child which it might cover & there was of course
The girl in question my own mother screaming in the wind

MURK

But of course you'd like to fuck Ophelia

Isn't that the whole point she asked
Her own skin as white as trout belly
& nearly as translucent in the liquid light
The moon let slide into her window

Just imagine me like that she said
The black-&-silver bed of slime beneath me
The sickening green water lapping at my thighs
But unlike your floating Ophelia

I'll be naked   my hair a damp red fan
& even the flowers of my nipples will calm
Beneath the lily pads as you bend above me
Anxious to spread open my legs until the whole

World of my death draws you to its embrace

PRISM (WHITE LIGHT)

Ice & the shadows of ice like the white scar

Of wind upon the world like the dust
Of polar flares strafing the St. Petersburg night

As the saint is laid again upon the grill of

Circumstance above the searing pearl ash until
Even the stars slowly drilling the sky rotate

In their boiling sockets & all hell breaks

Apart its howling white teeth its breath

Ruptured into the rapturous spectrum of
Pain by which we know the hues

Of our passage each one of us still assembling

The complicated palette (as in *Make me
A pallet on your floo*r) where sleep splinters

& the rage of the new day again coaxes us alive

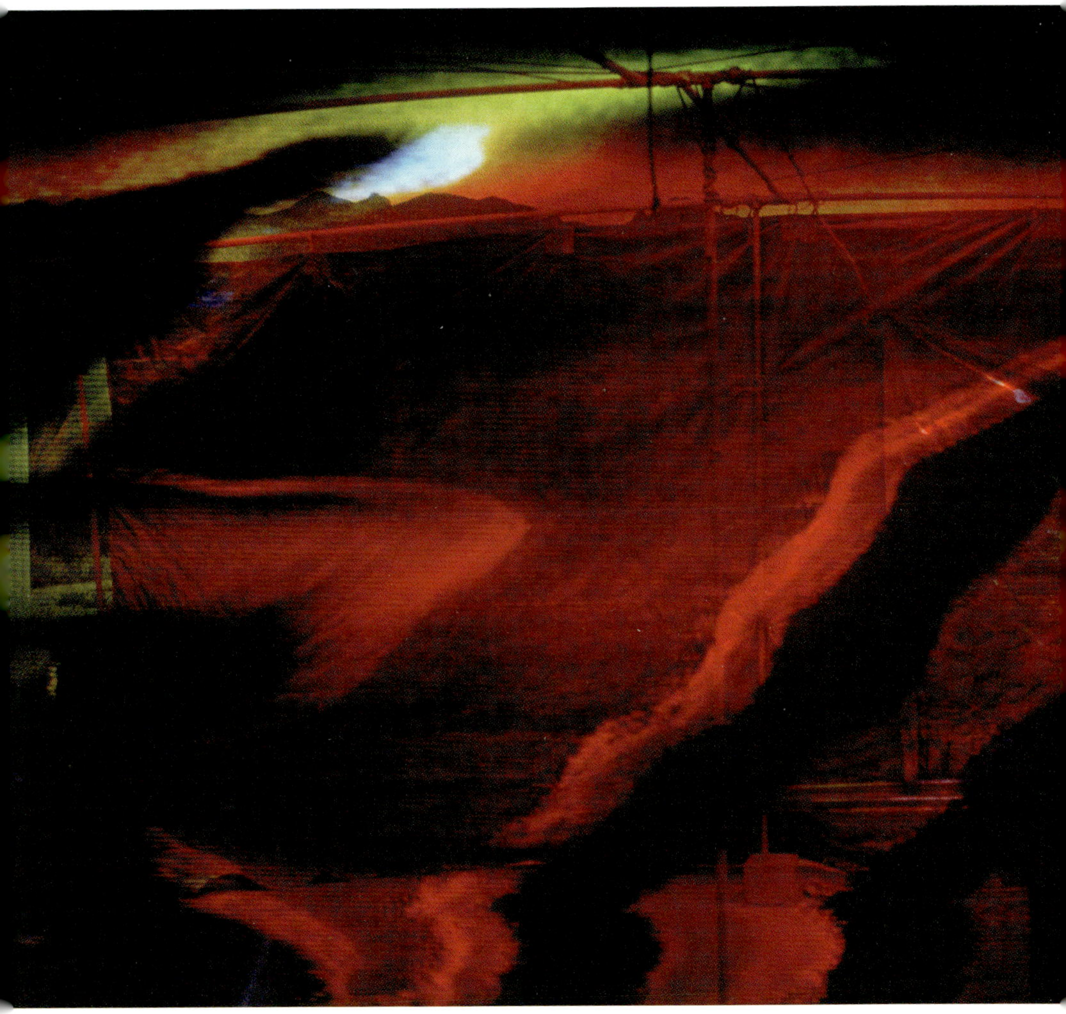

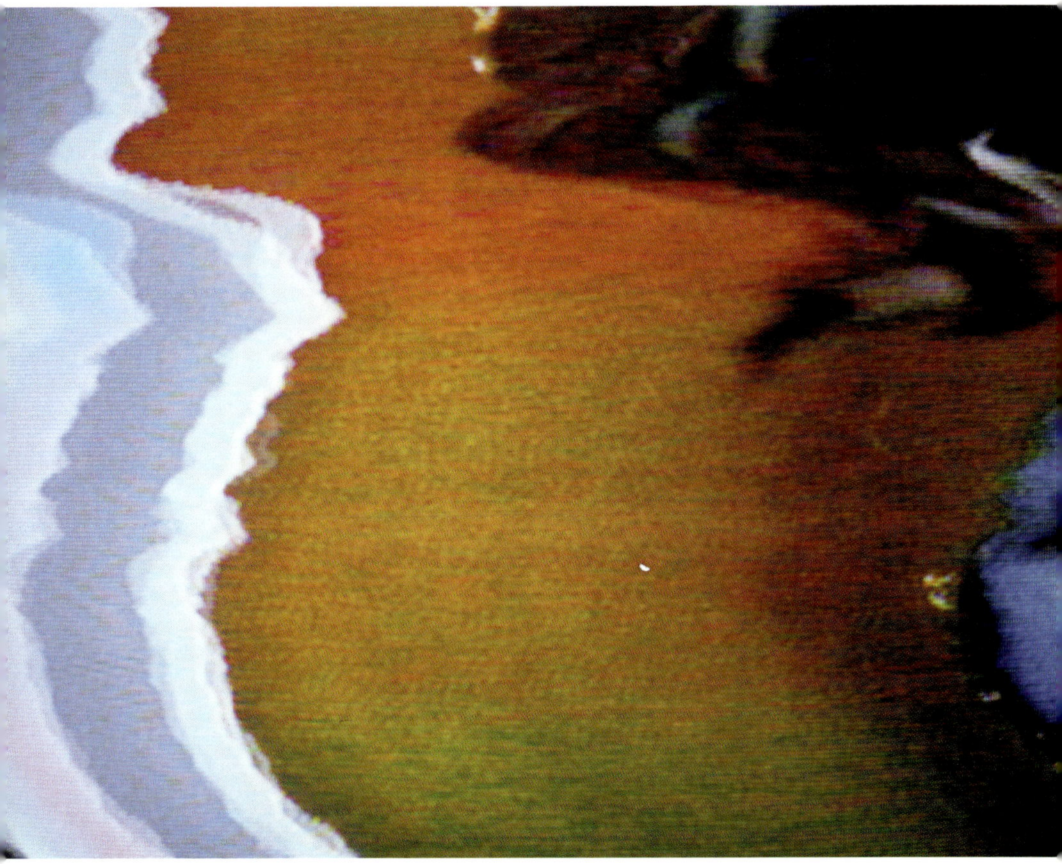

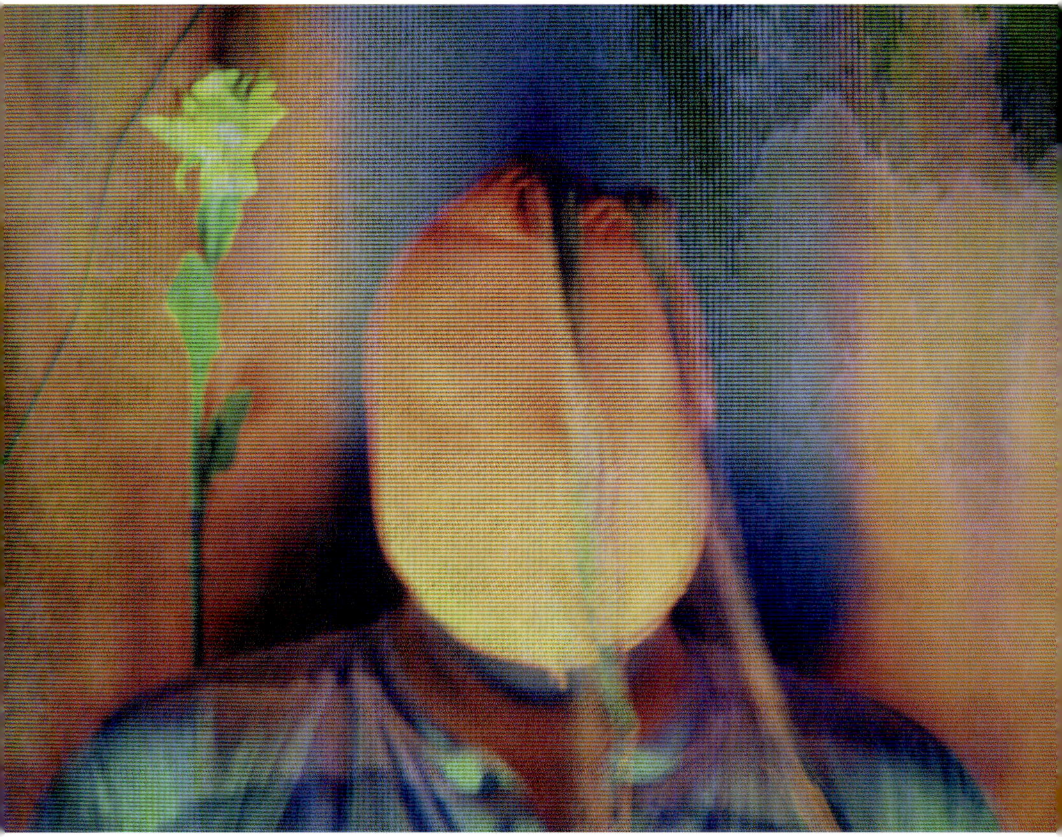

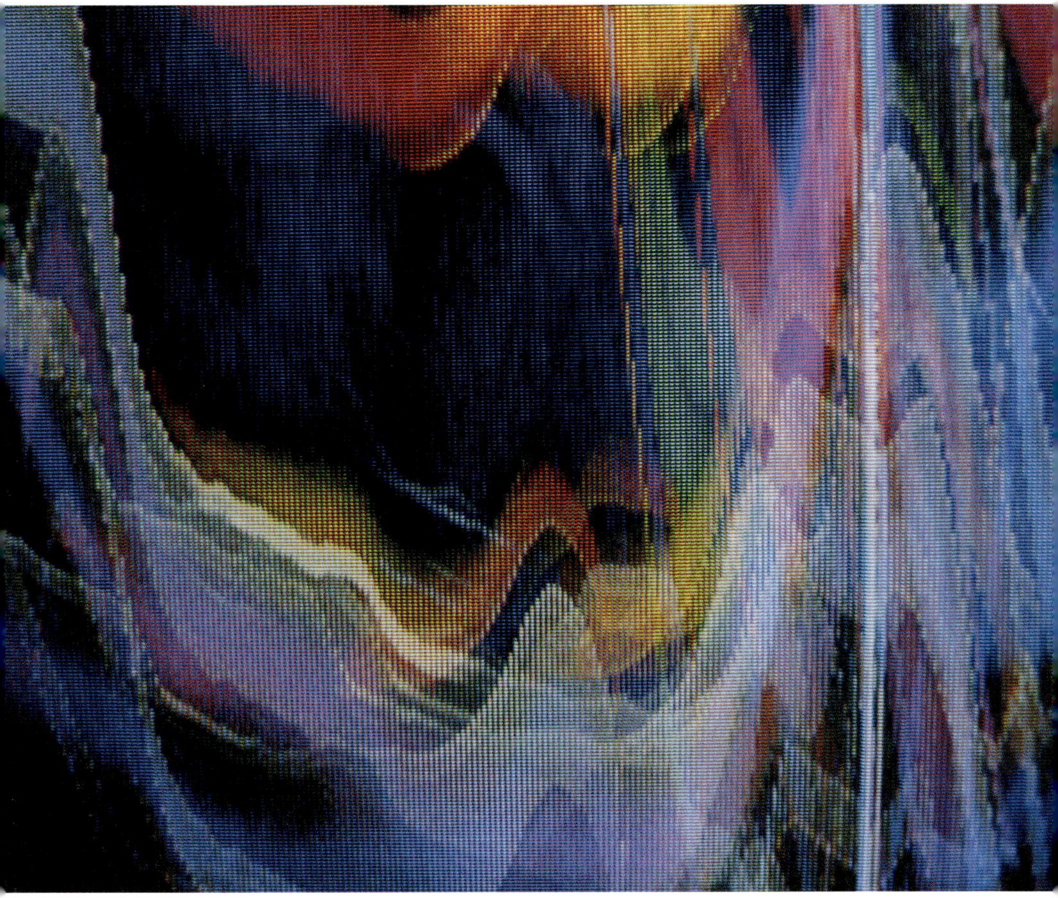